Charles Edward Andrews

Titanic Survivor

Charles Edward Andrews
Titanic Survivor

The Sea In My Blood

By

Marina Andrews

Copyright

Second Edition , August 2012
Title; Charles Edward Andrews ~ Titanic Survivor
Subtitle; The Sea In My Blood
Author; Marina Andrews
Email: Carlton12@sky.com
Copyright © 2012 *All rights reserved*

ISBN: 978-1-291-01233-0

Dedication

This Book Is Dedicated To;

My Grandfather

Charles Edward Andrews

And In Memory Of His Cousin;

George Edward Thomas Roberton

Table Of Contents

Preface

Marina Andrews is the granddaughter of Titanic survivor Charles Edward Andrews. Unfortunately, she never had the chance to know her grandfather, as sadly, he passed away two years before she was born. However, after studying old photographs and learning more from her family's collective recordings of Charlie and his colourful life at sea, Marina discovered she had created a mental vision of him; bringing her closer to the man she might once have known had he not passed away so soon. Marina feels proud of the way her grandfather coped through his long tough maritime career, sticking with it through thick and thin regardless of how difficult.

It was a kind of life definitely worth remembering, especially as it involved the great White Star liner RMS Titanic. But then realising over time, those memories of Charlie's distinct string of life-events would have gradually become completely forgotten.

This in turn - as well as Titanic's one hundredth anniversary year – sparked a great idea for a book! Filled with inspiration, Marina became motivated in creating a special keepsake for her family to prevent her grandfather's unique life fading away and ending in a pile of forgotten memories. Precious family memories of which Marina has compiled together, producing this unique family memento. A presentation which will now go on to preserve her grandfather's amazing life. Not only will Charlie's memoirs be there for her immediate family, but for his many future generations!

Surprisingly, as the word began to spread about her book, so did curiosity from the public. Many individuals were requesting copies before she had written a word! Marina knew there would be no going back once she had started. And being aware of the pressures of public interest, she decided to make her book available to everyone.

This is Marina's very first attempt at writing a book, and as much as she wanted to write it, her mind would also fill with all the usual feelings of concern, dreading how it would turn out or whether it would be good enough. Apart from wanting to write the book, Marina definitely wanted to illustrate some of it too. As a budding artist she has used her own illustrations from her own ideas, including the front cover.

Marina felt the book needed to emit that extra personal touch by creating the whole book in black and white to reflect the Era and times of Charlie's life.

Marina would not have been able to produce this book if her mother, Mary and certain helpful family members had not kept back the information and photos of her grandfather. I sincerely hope you enjoy reading this book, as much as Marina enjoyed writing it.

By Aston Cerexhe

Introduction

First, let me introduce you to my grandfather, Charles Edward Andrews, known then, as Charlie. More than a century ago, blue-eyed fair haired, Charlie, was just a normal lad from a very basic family lifestyle, who grew up with profound ambitions and dreams of becoming an able seaman. Strong willed Charlie went on to begin living his wildest dreams and ambitions of a very long maritime career, but nothing could have prepared him for the most harrowing experiences, and life threatening events that had transpired throughout Charlie's seafaring years. Although Charlie's life involved many tough and sad times, his life was also filled with lots of happy memories including fun, love and an amazing twenty year old promise with a very touching outcome! Although I never knew my grandfather Charlie, I feel as if I have come to know him through the creation of this book. Obviously, had Charlie not survived the Titanic

1

disaster, I would not have been here to write this book. And because he did, I feel privileged to have had the chance to preserve the life of this highly respected man who had such an exceptional life.

The Andrews Family

Dating back to the 13th century, the patriotic name Andrews originated from Scotland and arose from the baptismal name Andrew which, in Greek, means manly. The Andrews ancestry recorded in our family tree, dates back to (my grandfather) Charlie's great-great-great-grandfather, John Andrews born in a small village called Huish, amid the beautiful countryside of Wiltshire in around 1722. In 1746 John went on to marry his sweetheart Dinah Locke, they had a daughter and four sons, one of whom was Charlie's great-great-grandfather Henry, also born in Huish, Wiltshire in 1770. In April, 1790 Henry married Charlotte Tarrant; they had two daughters and three sons, one of whom was Charlie's great-grandfather Jeremiah, born in another small country village called Wilcot in Wiltshire, around 1803. Jeremiah moved to live in Portsea, Hampshire, to begin a new lease of life and in September 1826, he married Elizabeth Smithers. Jeremiah began his trade as a joiner and for several years he engaged as a member of the St Paul's Church choir in Southsea and became very well-known to the parish congregation for his fine bass voice and instrumental talent. When Jeremiah's wife Elizabeth reached her late thirties, she sadly passed away and two years later, lost their third child Thomas at the age of only thirteen. Sadness struck the family again for a third time, as just another year later, Jeremiah contracted Tuberculosis, after which shortly took his life; leaving their youngest three children orphaned. No one could possibly imagine the terrible grief those poor children must have suffered, having lost their brother and both parents over a short time.

On the 18th April in 1842, St Paul's orchestra arranged a special performance at the Beneficial Society's hall in Portsea. More than seventy members of the orchestra presented a grand concert of sacred music, in memory of their much respected member of the choir; talented vocalist, Jeremiah Andrews; Applying all funds received from the concert to the deceased's destitute orphans. The three children, Sarah aged just nine, Elizabeth, thirteen and George, eleven were all separated, each settling into a new life, living with other family members.

One of the three orphaned children, Jeremiah's eleven year old son, was Charlie's Grandfather George, born in Portsea, Hampshire in 1831. George worked hard at sea on the steamships becoming an able seaman working as a butcher. In 1854 George married Laura Glasse; they had seven children, of whom they tragically lost two; Arthur aged three and Herbert who was just two, in time burying both the children together in the old cemetery in Hill lane, Southampton.

One of George's other five children was Charlie's father, Henry Jeremiah, born in Southampton in 1857. In April 1869, when Henry was only twelve years old, his father George, accidentally drowned in an incident that occurred in Singapore, where his body remains buried. George was only thirty eight. Three years later, Henry's mother Laura re-married in 1872 to Edward Harvey. In 1881 Laura took over as licensee of the Beehive Hotel in Southampton with her husband Edward, who sadly later passed away in the September that same year. It seemed most of the family lived and worked there during the earlier part of their lives, including Henry Jeremiah. A year following her husband Edward's death, Laura married John Hall in Steyning, West Sussex, in 1882. Four years later Laura passed away and was

buried - Laura Anne Hall - with her two young sons Arthur and Herbert Andrews. In 1887, the license was taken over by George and Laura's daughter, Laura Elizabeth Andrews with her husband, Robert Okleford until her death in 1893.

Inevitably Henry decided to pursue a career at sea joining the Merchant Navy on board the White Star steamship Adriatic, until 1890. Also that year Henry entered a rowing contest, earning a gold medal with a white star, above reading the initials; S.S.M.A.C. Henry continued his seafaring career franchising a bar on the steamship Majestic until scrapped in 1914. Henry continued to later franchise the bar on the steamship Ionian at the Gallipoli landings with the

Anzac Forces in 1915 during the First World War.

Emily Ann Roberton

Liverpool

In 1879 Henry Jeremiah married Emily Roberton and first resided in Delamore St, Kirkdale, Merseyside. A few years later they moved a few streets away into Newark Street. On a cold bleak winter's day, Emily Andrews gave birth to her fifth child on the 18th of January, 1893. Emily and her husband Henry Jeremiah proudly named their new son Charles Edward. Charles would have become one of eight children, if it wasn't for the sad loss of his youngest brother Harry's twin at birth.

In those days, larger families of up to twelve children or more were the lifestyle, although huge families were common, so too were deaths during childbirth. At least one family experienced the devastating loss of a mother, child or more at birth. Birth control proved difficult then because it was unreliable and illegal. Heartbreaking losses through childbirth weren't the only causes that grieved our families. Sickness and poor health often took lives from all ages, even parents; leaving many children orphaned. In that period, through many generations, there were no immunisations available to protect against diseases such as; smallpox, whooping-cough, tuberculosis, measles etc. Widespread epidemics often swept across towns and villages affecting thousands of families. Overcrowded homes and poor sanitation contributed towards infection, causing such illnesses as; dysentery and diarrhoea. Many people appeared thin, suffering weight loss through a lack of nourishment, contributing to other diseases, such as scurvy. Like many others, through the years, the Andrews family also saw their share of famine, sickness and loss.

By the time Charlie was born, the family was living in Bedford Road, Liverpool - where Charlie spent the early part of his childhood. As with all children of that era, Charlie was born and bred into the life where he and other children were dressed like little adults and treated as adults. Our modern "teenager" of today did not exist then. The Andrews siblings appeared much more grown up and mature at a younger age and acted in a more serious manner. Without protest and with respect, Charlie and his siblings accepted the responsibility in their share of a long list of arduous household duties.

For Boys, their future occupations were considered a high priority and most important, thus expecting them to work hard, and study well at school. It was less important for the young women as later, most of them - even as young as sixteen - became mothers, wives and homemakers. When Charlie's two sisters, Amy and Laura were old enough to raise a family; they already knew how to run and manage a household of their own. It was common to see children, especially boys, working at an early age, as young as six or even younger and

10

bringing in a wage to help support the family. As opposed to nowadays, potentially every member of the household did their bit accepting the ethics of everyday hardships, however tiring it was.

Times proved even tougher for the Andrews siblings when schooldays began. Like most of us, Charlie would remember the first time he started school. Those Victorian memories of his early primary school days appeared somewhat unpleasant. Charlie had no choice, but to grin and bear his new school, a school with a daunting appearance that presented grim looking classrooms with ugly bare walls. There was not a coloured picture in sight, and absolutely nothing to welcome young children into school.

But as hard and meticulous school life was for the children, Charlie and his siblings settled in well and worked hard, trying to make the best of school time. Charlie's character soon proved popular at school, friendships developed over time, and if any of his pals fell into difficulties, Charlie would be the one they would always call on.

Keeping in check with the incredibly strict teachers and tight disciplinary rules, was far from easy in those days. Punishment by cane was a regular ritual for disobedient pupils. Without a doubt, stern controls in schools then certainly contributed towards conditioning the children to later grow into respectful adults. When some children were as young as twelve years old, they were already leaving school to find employment.

Unlike the rest of his brothers and sisters, there appeared a distinctive quality in Charlie. Being so mature at a young age he developed a remarkable sense of independence, with a caring passion for people and the world; a sensible and unique nature of character that would help him sail through life, face and challenge the toughest of times. Even at home, Charlie's own life wasn't always easy and

11

because there were so many family members, Charlie's mother, Emily, had no choice but to keep a tight shipshape routine at their home in Bedford Road.

Bedford Road in Walton - known then as Walton-On-The-Hill - ran in a line straight down to the Liverpool piers. Come, rain, snow or shine, it was there that Charlie and his brothers would race in a mad dash of excitement, down to the end of the long road to the quayside. On many a day, they would watch in a joyful trance of fascination as their father, Henry, would sail into port on the SS Majestic. As young as the boys were, they held much pride and respect for their father; the excited lads always looked forward to him coming home from sea. The limited time they could spend with their father and the family together, before it was time for him to depart, felt very precious to them.

Once again, their father's time to return to his ship soon came. Filled with sorrow the boys hated waving him off, it was clearly a disheartening sight as the brothers' sadness loomed. Charlie and his brothers would stay and watch as the SS Majestic would gradually steam away from the pier. With dropped sullen faces obscured by their cloth caps, the idle lads would slowly turn back with their heads drooped, wandering aimlessly home from the pier. By the time their mother Emily had preoccupied their tiny minds with various tasks around the house, the moments of despair would have soon faded.

Their lives were very basic, like everyone else who lived in the street. Although the house was quite roomy, it had no bathroom and the toilet was housed outside in a cold brick room, infested with small creepy crawlies and dusty cobwebs. However, Emily always made sure her children were kept clean. Every night by the warm open fireside, she would wash her children in an old tin bath, ensuring their nails were scrubbed and kept trim; she made all of her children wash thoroughly, even behind their ears. In that period, that is how it was, there were no luxuries like we have nowadays. The children certainly weren't spoilt; they had nothing, and wanted for nothing, all they had was their own amusement, which surprisingly with a bit of imagination created a lot of fun and enjoyment to the children in their time. But of course growing up in that way of life, they didn't know any different.

The four brothers, Alex, Charlie, Harry and Bert became familiar faces with the regular seamen down at the pier, especially Charlie. The lads' mad frantic waves and cheeky grinning faces were a pleasant welcoming sight for the tired rugged looking seamen returning home after weeks away at sea. The boys thoroughly enjoyed spending many hours hanging out at the piers, sometimes basking in the scorching heat on hot summer days. Occasionally the older lads would cool off, taking pleasure diving off the quayside, while the merrily amused youngsters, would just sit attentive, absorbing every moment that passed at the port. Although weeks away from seeing their father again and sometimes thousands of miles apart, the quayside was the only place that made the boys feel closer to him. Captured by the strong inspiration of the sea, with their desired future in mind, Henry's boys could only wait longingly in hope that one day they could follow in their father's footsteps and work for the White Star Line. Of the four brothers, Charlie, Harry and Bert together formed a special bond always looking out for each other, but Charlie and Harry became the closest; Charlie was the one they would rely on and look up to.

Southampton

In 1907 the White Star Line transferred its main port from Liverpool to Southampton. In the same year, when Charlie was aged fourteen, the Andrews family followed suit, moving from their home in Liverpool and settling into a house in Imperial Avenue, Shirley for a new lease of life living in the southern City of Southampton. Charlie's sister Amy, at just sixteen years old, decided to stay, got married, started a family and continued to live in Liverpool.

The four brothers remained as close as ever sharing time together, getting to know their new surroundings in their new hometown of Shirley. The children soon found new friends, and would spend some days out walking for miles, with maybe a jam sandwich stuffed in one frayed jacket pocket and a piece of fruit tucked inside the other. Sometimes they would be given a penny or half to spend on a treat - if they were lucky! Occasionally there would be simple errands to run for their mother or a small local job that would bring in some extra pennies. Even then, there was always something to occupy the lads' forever active minds, the children made their own pleasure when venturing out and about; whether it was building a cart from old broken prams and scraps found dumped on the streets, or the unlimited imaginative games of adventure.

Those days were considered much safer than today; Emily had fewer concerns of where her children went, for how long, or worries of any danger.

Discovering a new dock in Southampton where the White Star Line steamships started to sail in and out was another big adventure for the Andrew brothers. It wasn't long before the boys' faces were again a recognised sight among their father's fellow crewmembers. The lads always thoroughly enjoyed the occasional days that they could accompany their father home on the trams from the Docks, all sat listening, and captivated by the tales of his seafaring ventures, some good and others not so good, but they were all true.

Another noticeable quality in Charlie was his profound passion for swimming. Charlie seemed to have a thing about water, whether it was swimming in it, or sailing on it, he loved it. In total confidence, Charlie practiced often; he took to water like a fish and was always eager to take part in regular swimming events. Building strength he developed his unique skills, showing off his natural ability in the water. Charlie took much pride competing with his school team and later won a silver championship cup for the Southampton School of Swimming.

Charlie's love for the water and his competence as a swimmer later opened up other opportunities to train as a lifeguard and swimming instructor. Only later would Charlie realise that his potential fitness gained through swimming, would one day contribute immensely towards easing pressures off hard-hitting future events.

Ambitions and goals weren't Charlie's only hopeful visions in mind. Those wishes and dreams of becoming a seaman for the White Star Line were not far from becoming reality for Charlie, when in 1908 at just fifteen, his father, Henry, found him work aboard the White Star's steamships in the Southampton Docks. To become an able seaman Charlie needed certain qualifications, including commitment and hard work. Charlie knew this is what he had always wanted and had waited for a long time, so from bare-knuckle to heel for the first two years as an apprentice steward, Charlie dedicated himself to working long tiring hours, training hard to earn his right to become a proud and admired able seaman.

There was no financial pay in return but instead Charlie was provided with clothes, good meals and a hard bunk in a tiny bare cabin. As tough and tiring as it was, every day, from the very first passenger rising to the last to retire for the night, Charlie along with others his age, were continually on the go. However, he did discover there were good tips to be had! As with all seamen, Charlie and his many seafaring relatives worked hard out at sea and endured many hazards of the ocean, including all climates, however rough. Seamen were isolated from their families back home ashore for long periods of time, maybe weeks, and months or even longer. On board ship, officers kept a strict disciplinary routine for the crew, and survival meant every seaman had to be physically and mentally strong enough to withstand the eventual stresses of maritime labour.

On the 20th September 1911, departing from Southampton and bound for New York; Charlie encountered and survived his first major incident at sea, working as a steward aboard Titanic's sister ship, RMS Olympic. Charlie had not long returned to Southampton on the Olympic's previous crossing from New York, but on this occasion the events that took place were quite other than ordinary. During an attempt to sail the same path of water off the coast of the Isle of Wight, the Olympic collided with British warship, HMS Hawke. Pulled in by the suction of the Olympic, the warship slammed into her side. The impact was great causing major damage to both ships. It certainly wasn't the best of ships to collide with, for the Hawke was fitted with a battering ram – purposely placed for ramming enemy ships. However fortunately for the Olympic, the impact was not as massive as Titanic's but massive enough to cause two of Olympic's compartments to flood, including some degree of damage to the propeller and shaft. But, however wounded the Olympic was, Captain Edward Smith just about managed to get her back safely to Southampton, then on to Belfast for repair. On the 29th November that same year Charlie was back, serving on board the Olympic after the ships quick recovery.

Four long years of hard maritime labour passed for Charlie, and he was now a fit nineteen year old. He had experienced nearly every niche as a trainee steward, meeting every passenger including - in those times - the kindest and most generous of the poor, to the downright meanest and egotistical of the rich! Regardless of passenger class or distinction, the sea was now Charlie's new life, although demanding, he cherished every passing moment!

Charlie's Replacement Discharge Book

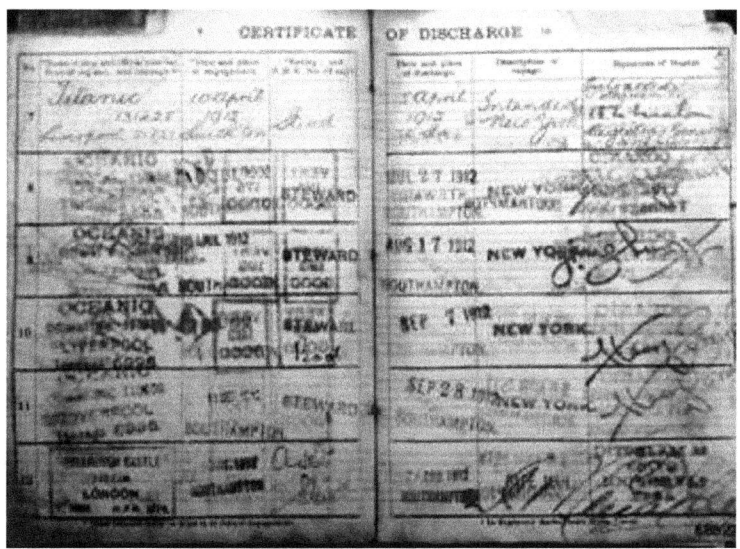

Original, lost with Titanic

Always Stamped, Very Good!

RMS Titanic

Titanic

In early April 1912 it wasn't long before Charlie found a new and more adventurous employment, signing on to White Star's luxurious steamship Titanic, as an assistant second class saloon steward. Charlie also managed to find a position - as a second class assistant steward - for his cousin, George Edward Thomas Roberton, born from Charlie's mother's side of the family; He too was nineteen years old, and followed the sea. Since then, the family had moved home several times in and around Southampton, but by the time Charlie joined Titanic he had been living at their new address in Millbrook Road.

On that fine spring day on Wednesday 10th of April 1912, it was a glorious time for the people of Southampton. The whole Andrews family ventured down to the Dock amid the parting emotions of the crowds. They wanted to give Charlie and his cousin George a memorable send-off as the cousins began their new employment working aboard the magnificent new White Star liner, Royal Mail Steamship Titanic on her maiden voyage.

Pushing on with heightened excitement through the people to catch a better view of the ship, the family discovered the most breathtaking sight ever imagined. Before their widening eyes, looking up at the enormous liner beginning to move slowly away, they couldn't help but to stare with amazement at the emotional reception of euphoric joy and excitement. Southampton's new passengers had gathered leaning out from most decks - responding to the farewells – displayed a continuous flowing movement of hands, hats, gloves, and handkerchiefs, waving them frantically back at the spectators on the quayside.

Unlike any other, the steamship resembled a floating palace laced with the utmost of luxury. Without a doubt, one would definitely have had to experience for real, the distinct sight of the finest steamship ever built, to comprehend the value and quality of such magnificence. The Royal Mail Steamship Titanic certainly lived up to its name, as it paraded out along the Solent emitting an impressive spectacle on the Southampton skyline; depicting an object of sheer determination and ambition in its design. Remembering too, with appreciation and understanding, the blood, sweat, and tears of grief that went into building the incredibly massive ship. It is almost impossible to imagine the complete pride and fulfillment the labourers and craftsmen of the time must have felt having built such a stunning vessel, regardless of the pittance they were paid in return.

Once aboard the beautiful liner, the lads had settled in early that fresh morning. Charlie and George's duties started almost immediately; there was no time for unnecessary banter. Time proved precious for the crew, who were expected to provide a fine service, serving in a skilful and orderly manner to all passengers on board. Joining Titanic was straightforward for Charlie as he had already gained steward experience on previous White Star ships, such as the Oceanic. Most of the crew employed on Titanic, had previously experienced working at sea. At the time, many ships were stranded in Southampton's port due to the coal strike. This meant a vast number of seamen without work, had signed onto Titanic, including a seaman who would have been our third family crew member, but a mysterious dream occurred. The most fascinating thing about it, was when able seaman, Harry Hughes was scheduled to sign onto Titanic.

Just before the ship was due to leave, his wife Florence had a terrifying nightmare that Titanic had sunk. The nightmare had upset her so much; Florence had begged and begged, pleading with her husband Harry not to go. Luckily in the end he gave in to his concerned wife's pleas and decided to stay behind. The man in question was Charlie's brother Harry's father in law; Harry Hughes. Although he was rather spooked, he was certainly glad that he had stayed behind.

On Titanic, Charlie's job involved several responsibilities as an assistant saloon steward. His role included keeping dining areas clean, handling food, waiting tables, setting and clearing tables. Other tasks would involve sanitising the galley and pantry and removing rubbish ensuring all of his duties ordered from the Chief Steward were kept in check. In particular, it was important for stewards to tend to passengers with extreme care. As with all stewards, Charlie had to present himself with the highest standard of cleanliness with a smartly groomed appearance upholding a polite manner of conduct at all times.

Slowly moving on, that Wednesday afternoon, through

Southampton waters, Titanic experienced a close call, almost colliding with the liner New York, causing an hour's delay in reaching Cherbourg. Titanic later showed off her splendour as she docked at Cherbourg's pier for a short stay, soon setting sail again, heading for her final call at Queenstown (now Cobh) in Southern Ireland for the remaining passengers. On route to the open ocean of the North Atlantic, the weather looked hopeful with a calm flat sea reflected under a blue sky. Over the following few days, passengers would take great pleasure relishing the fine cuisine and absorbing the jolly entertainment on board. Some would take a casual stroll after mealtimes, admiring the superior beauty of the ship, while others sat relaxing with a nap. But many passengers took pleasure soaking up the glorious atmosphere on the decks, appreciating the supreme smoothness of the journey.

White Star Line's RMS Titanic was considered by some the "ship of dreams" and was the largest and most prestigious ship of that time. For the two thousand two hundred or so passengers aboard, the journey should have been the ultimate dream of a lifetime, but most unfortunately on that Sunday night of the 14th April 1912, the wonderful dream gradually began to fade and a dark unforgettable nightmare was about to unfold.

There was no boat drill held on that unfortunate Sunday. In the evening Captain Smith was at dinner in the saloon. Afterwards he left the saloon to sit with his party in the Companionway where the orchestra played. The Captain was noticeably very cheerful and appeared most contented in his moments of pleasure whilst socialising. In fact everyone on board seemed to be having a great time.

Charlie was on watch that fine spring evening, after which he gladly returned to his quarters shortly before eleven for a well deserved nights rest. While stretching out on his bunk relaxing, Charlie began to feel the pressures release from a tiring days work. Charlie took some moments to reflect back on some of the most amusing events of the day. Happily contented with the trip and his hectic days schedule, Charlie's mind began to fade with sleepiness.

But then, out of the blue, something startled him, and he awoke. Charlie had only been in his quarters for just less than an hour, when he and his crew-mates - asleep in their quarters - were disturbed by a slight shudder of the ship. Curious, Charlie got up from his bunk, and went on deck with another steward to see if anything had happened. He walked about for a bit but saw nothing unusual, so returned to his bunk. Charlie then heard a sudden rush of water, which he thought was a bit odd. So he got up again - dressing quickly to leave. No sooner than Charlie was ready, the order came;" All hands on deck". Charlie went up onto the boat deck and shortly stood by his lifeboat, the air felt deadly cold. As he stood around waiting in the freezing air for the next instruction, he wished he had dressed much warmer.

Charlie had only been informed by another fellow steward that morning before breakfast which boat was his. Lifeboat number sixteen was Charlie's assigned boat; this was - one of the sixteen wooden boats - stowed on hinged wooden chocks, secured by ropes connected to a davit, situated on the boat deck on the port side of the ship with the other even numbered boats - two to sixteen - installed from the bow to the stern. The sixteen lifeboats were built to safely carry sixty five people. Just as with Titanic, the handicraft and quality of the lifeboats reflected a professional standard; each boat was constructed using fixed wooden planks of yellow pine. Other parts of the lifeboats were made from elm and oak.

That Sunday evening, on the boat deck, more people started to gather. Standing around waiting curiously, no one seemed to show any apprehension or fear because there were no signs to indicate such a disaster had occurred. Most of the passengers and crew on board that fateful night were unaware of the fact that there were not enough lifeboats to save all souls from the luxury steamship. Lifeboat chitchat seemed to be an inappropriate subject for what was deemed an unsinkable ship; at the slightest thought, one would have shrugged in full belief and confidence that the liner was, indeed, unsinkable.

The night of the sinking went on to prove just how much self-assurance the passengers showed during the first hour or so after Titanic struck the iceberg. With no concern or panic shown, passengers displayed a calm and relaxed approach, some even refusing to leave the warmth and comfort of the ship. With reluctance, most of the passengers only stepped into lifeboats simply because they were instructed to and some were curious to see what would happen! Only later did they learn the horrifying reality that Titanic had struck an iceberg which had unfortunately sealed her fate.

Iceberg

As beautiful and as innocent as icebergs appear, they can present a deadly danger, especially just below sea level to vessels crossing the vast North Atlantic Ocean. Merging together forming fields of ice; floating chunks of frozen fresh water do display some remarkable sights during the daytime and create some amazing colourful illusions at night. The iceberg that Titanic collided with would probably have been aged around five thousand years old. Breaking free from its spectacular glacial habitat on the west coast of Greenland - at a snail's pace - the iceberg would very slowly creep across the glacier, making its way towards the Atlantic Ocean. The huge berg would then continue on its way passing through "Iceberg Alley" close to the seafaring City of St John's, in Newfoundland. Eventually the berg would reach the vast North Atlantic Ocean, drifting at a rate of approximately 0.05mph and continuing on southwards merging with a floating field of ice. The huge towering obstruction would have finally drifted into place; laying silently in wait, right in the direct path of the doomed liner, Royal Mail Steamship Titanic.

Lifeboat Sixteen

Having remembered what he had learned from attending his boat drills, mustered in New York, Charlie took his approach to the situation with a professional and calm manner. He first assisted by helping women and children into the lifeboat, and as he did so, he felt an undercurrent of raw emotion stir within as he could hear the tender moments of families parting. Charlie remained calm and continued to fill the boat, concealing his personal concerns and feelings, until the officers believed the lifeboat was full.

An officer then turned to Charlie and asked if he would take an oar. Charlie obligingly accepted, climbed into the lifeboat, put the rowlocks in place and took position. The lifeboat was then slowly lowered into the icy water from its davit. Once the lifeboat hit the water's surface with a thud, the crew began to row away from the doomed ship. It was the eighth boat to leave Titanic, at a time around 1.35 am.

Further on out, about half a mile from Titanic, they had met up with another lifeboat filled with women, and in need of an oarsman. And so, from lifeboat sixteen one of the crewmen was transferred across into the other boat to assist with rowing. Just at that moment, cries could be heard from the vicinity of the ship. Charlie could just about see - through a blackened mist - the remaining half of Titanic pitched above sea level. A small sound was heard coming from the ship; Charlie thought it may have been one of the boilers, but he couldn't be certain.

Altogether dazed, floating out on the icy cold dark ocean, all they could do was sit quietly and wait, watching in horror while the remaining lifeboats were being filled. The survivors continued to watch as Titanic slip slowly and deeper below the surface. All stunned with bewilderment by the terrible sight, no one could utter a single word. Their minds instantly froze over in shock, as their very short moments of disbelief, were horrifyingly shattered by the distinct blow of reality.

When the final moment came, at around 2.20am, everywhere around suddenly became very darkened and misty as Titanic's bright illuminating lights fused. The cruel bleak icy sea took many souls with Titanic swallowing them down into the freezing cold depths of the North Atlantic Ocean.

Amid the murky blackness, a strange atmosphere around the lifeboats portrayed an eerie calm, except in the far distance. Charlie and the remaining survivors in the boat could hear bone chilling screams and pleading cries from the helpless terrified people thrashing around in the perishing seawater. It seemed for a moment to go on forever, but it really didn't take very long. The movements and pleas of the ones suffering rapidly became weaker and weaker, until finally their sobs quietly faded into a gripping empty silence.

Deeply embedded inside their memory, those bitter cries of torture would no doubt go on to haunt every survivor's mind throughout the rest of their lives. In spite of everything, the seven hundred or so survivors that safely filled the lifeboats still remained profoundly troubled by the uncertain fate of their futures; nobody could predict where any of them would end up.

Along with the rest of the crew, Charlie battled on hard against the freezing cold, struggling to keep a focus on what seemed, an infinite North Atlantic Sea.

They were all now beginning to suffer the full force of the sharp frigid sea air. The severe penetrating chill cut in deep like a sharp blade through the few layers of Charlie's clothing that covered his numb body. As Charlie pushed himself on with effort, he began to realise the distinct possibility that they may never be rescued alive. As the boat drifted further through the early hours of that spring April morning, their minds became plagued by agonizing thoughts of suffering a very possible and unpleasant death at sea. In despair and fearing the worst, they would often pray to god, begging for mercy through tears of sorrow. Their pale faces would look up with tearful eyes to see the lucid heavens displaying a beautiful cosmic array of twinkling stars.

Various mysterious lights were seen out on the ocean that night. Raising their despairing hopes now and then, the crew would attempt to sail towards one, but no rescue ships came. As minutes and hours slowly passed by, the night seemed endless, it really felt unreal just as if they were all living an intense nightmare; a nightmare that could never be forgotten.

In a seemingly timeless world, miles from nowhere, and feeling completely helpless, the crew would often tire from rowing and rest. Aimlessly in flow with the tide, the lifeboat continued to rock with freedom on the water, carrying the weakened survivors who mournfully waited, staring spellbound by the images of stalking icebergs as their vessel silently drifted on through fields of ice. Miles and miles of icy water is all they could manage to see, it was just as if all the land had completely disappeared and the world was entirely covered in boundless oceans!

Just the thoughts of those fears were enough to haunt their delirious minds forever; and was also very frightening to know that at any moment the sea could just snatch their lives away. The profound stress of the situation had finally set in causing most of the suffering victims to doze, due to feeling rather sleepy in response to the exposure of extremely low temperatures. The crew always tried to keep the survivor's insights positive, by diverting their minds away from the terrifying grim reality.

Over many hours on the bleak ocean, even Mother Nature herself had her natural calls at such an inconvenient time, placing dignities to shame as pennies became inevitably spent. Still, with unwavering faith the group sat trembling amid their extremely cold uncomfortable damp clothes, while they struggled for comfort huddling as one for shelter. Although the survivors had no clue of their outcome, holding onto all hope they continued with mite to remain strong in mind.

As the morning tides changed, struggling against the swaying boat through the latter morning hours started to prove more and more difficult for the crew, as the strength of the Atlantic waves began lashing in turn, like vicious whips against each side of the boat.

Charlie's thoughts turned to the suffering women and few small children in his boat, and as a family man it really broke his heart to see their fear, pain and suffering. Without a doubt a in his mind, however tough or painstaking it was for himself, Charlie's main priorities had kicked in, automatically placing their lives before his own. Even with the little remaining strength he had left, whenever the possibility of a ship was in sight, Charlie would power himself on for the suffering women and children, combining his full determination along with the other crewmen.

Fighting wearily against the sheer bitterness of the sea breeze and some of the now harsher waves, Charlie tried so hard to row in time with the other struggling crewmen. It was excessively hard work, and the most distressing, no other vessel or event in Charlie's life would ever compare to the long intense time he had experienced on lifeboat sixteen.

Surprisingly for the survivors, time did eventually pass that crisp April morning. And as the morning skies grew steadily lighter over - what resembled - an ocean of glass, an eye piercing sun suddenly peeped over the horizon, projecting its impressive warm rays displaying a beautiful shimmering reflection stretching across the broad glassy sea.

A welcoming dawn had finally arrived and visibility had dramatically improved. It was an impressive sight, and as the group began to peer through their blurry eyes to look, they became aware of something else out on the ocean.

A glow was noticed in the distance that Monday morning, heading towards it, the crew and passengers anxiously prepared themselves with all faith. Suddenly the survivors just couldn't believe what they were seeing, as the familiar glow drew closer. A distinct silhouette appeared, before them, becoming much clearer and a more obvious sight. With all eyeballs firmly fixed on the unbelievable vision, nothing could have been more welcoming - as the moment the Carpathia finally came into view.

As the grateful survivors were overly welcomed on board the ship, in an instant their fears and worries had finally dispersed. They couldn't find the words, if any, to describe how the immense relief had felt to be aboard the Carpathia. The survivors were all treated very much like royalty, a noticeable high standard of previously organised provisions were generously applied to all the remaining survivors, including dry clothes and blankets, hot soups and drinks. It was evidently clear, the captain and crew of Carpathia took a tremendous amount of care and support placing every part of their heart and soul into the rescue of Titanic's survivors.

Even though the survivors rescued were gratefully relieved to be finally safe, little did they realise, they were actually blessed with a second stroke of luck. Bearing in mind, that when Titanic sent out its distress signal, it had sent an incorrect position, but if the Titanic had sent its correct position. Carpathia may never have found the lifeboats until much later, if at all, and the freezing weather and conditions would have inflicted a dramatic effect on the survivors' health which meant they would possibly have perished at sea from hypothermia.

At Home

Back home in England the rapid spread of the devastating news of Titanic's sinking hit hard, especially for the City of Southampton.

Charlie's family had heard too but they had no idea whether Charlie or George had survived or not. The daily despair and sleepless nights of not knowing was not only an emotional nightmare for the Andrews family, but for all families who had friends and relatives aboard Titanic. Dreading the worse, Emily had told Charlie's brother Harry to stay home from school and instead go down to the White Star Offices in Southampton every single day from his home in Millbrook Road, to check on the latest bulletins until there was news, hopefully listing that Charlie and his cousin George were safe. Out of respect, most homes throughout Southampton kept their curtains drawn. The distressing news of the disaster continued to stun thousands of city residents. Shocked beyond absolute disbelief, the people of Southampton were so confused, for they had highly regarded Titanic as being "unsinkable".

On the day young Harry returned home to his mother with the latest news, the devastating truth hit the Andrews family, whilst they were overly relieved to learn that Charlie had survived; the family were also deeply devastated over the sad loss of Charlie's poor cousin George who drowned. Not even words could explain how Charlie must have felt, having found the position on Titanic for George in the first place.

New York

On the 15th April 1912 on the west side of Manhattan in New York City, the luxury steamship Titanic was destined to dock at the White Star pier number fifty nine, after her long maiden voyage across the North Atlantic Ocean from Southampton, England. One can only now imagine the ecstatic welcoming reception there would have been, as Titanic slowly came in to dock at the quayside for her first time. Streaming banners and flowing ribbons, crowds cheering and screaming, waving franticly with excitement as eyes fill with tears of joy! Passengers would set foot from the luxuriant liner, faces gleaming with pride and excitement as each one absorbingly cherished the moment of fulfillment. But sadly for Titanic and those poor unfortunate souls she took with her, it just wasn't to be. For frantic relatives and anxious friends at home, time must indeed have felt like a lifetime of anguish, desperately waiting for news during those few days it took for the Carpathia to finally reach New York.

On the 18th April1912,Charles Edward Andrews - one of the seven hundred or so remaining survivors rescued by Carpathia went on to set foot in New York City; A City's port that would significantly reminisce those dreadful memories throughout Charlie's life. Many lives were lost during the sinking of Titanic. Not only did the disaster end their futures, but instantly changed the lives of others. For Charlie, life continued on the same path, a path just beyond the beginning of his long career still following the sea. As a young crew member with a few years of tough maritime experience behind him; New York later became a prime locality where Charlie would devote much of his social time.

(Copy)

UNITED STATES OF AMERICA.

Congress of the United States.

To C. Andrews

—————————————————————————————— Greeting:

Pursuant to lawful authority, YOU ARE HEREBY COMMANDED to appear before the Sub Committee on Commerce of the Senate of the United States, on Monday April 22nd 1912 at 10:30 o'clock A.M. at their Committee Room #41 of Senate Office Building Washington D.C., then and there to testify what you may know relating to the subject-matters under consideration by said Committee.

Hereof fail not, as you will answer your default under the pains and penalties in such cases made and provided.

TO DANIEL M. RANSDELL, Sergeant-at-Arms of the Senate of the United States, to serve and return.

Given under my hand, by order of the Committee, this 20th day of April, in the year of our Lord one thousand nine hundred and twelve.

William Alden Smith
Chairman, Committee on Commerce.

On the 20th April in New York, Charlie was served a subpoena. Summoned as a witness Charlie was required to provide evidence in relation to the Titanic disaster. He was ordered to remain in New York until after his testimony which took place on the seventh day of the Senate Inquiry at 10.30am at the Waldorf-Astoria Hotel in New York City on the 22nd April 1912. He had no means to provide for himself, as the crew's pay had been stopped after the sinking, so therefore he had no choice but to rely on generous hand outs. For the couple of weeks or so that Charlie was confined in New York he would utilise the time with his crewmates, still in a state of shock and in anticipation of the impending inquiry.

41

Testimony

United States Senate Enquiry

Day 7

Testimony of C E Andrews (Am.Inq, P622)

(The witness was sworn by Senator Bourne)

Senator Bourne; "Please state your name, age & occupation"
Mr Andrews; "C E Andrews, age 19 125 Millbrook Road, Southampton, Occupation Steward"
Senator Bourne; "How long have you followed the sea"?
Mr Andrews; "This is my fourth year sir".
Senator Bourne; "How long have you been a steward"?
Mr Andrews; "I have been a steward now sir – this is my fourth year sir"
Senator Bourne; "When you started to sea, you started in the capacity of a steward did you"?
Mr Andrews; "Yes sir officer's steward."
Senator Bourne; "Were you on the Titanic on her maiden voyage"?
Mr Andrews; "Yes sir"
Senator Bourne; "When did you join the ship"?
Mr Andrews; "On Wednesday morning sir, the day of the sailing,

the 10th April".

Senator Bourne; "And you were with her up until the time of the catastrophe"?

Mr Andrews; "Yes sir"

Senator Bourne; "Were you allotted to any of the lifeboats or emergency boats or rafts"?

Mr Andrews; "I do not know anything about that sir, but a friend of mine, a steward second class, he told me to go and see what my boat was, on Sunday morning, and just before breakfast he came back and told me it was No 16".

Senator Bourne; "Did you go to No 16 at the time of the accident"?

Mr Andrews; "I did, sir".

Senator Bourne; "What officer was in charge of No 16"?

Mr Andrews; "I could not tell you what officer, sir".

Senator Bourne; "Was it an officer or one of the petty officers"?

Mr Andrews; "An officer, sir".

Senator Bourne; "Had you sailed with the White Star Line prior to this voyage"?

Mr Andrews; "Yes sir, I had been with the White Star Line just four years".

Senator Bourne; "And your service has been with them"?

Mr Andrews; "Yes, Sir".

Senator Bourne; "In all of the four years' service as steward with them, have you participated in any of their fire or boat drills"?

Mr Andrews; "Yes, sir".

Senator Bourne; "How often have they been held"?

Mr Andrews; "Well, they have been held on Sunday. They muster in New York or hold Muster in New York and there is one on the Sunday home sir".

Senator Bourne; "During your voyages, have you held any of these drills"?

Mr Andrews; "Yes, sir".

Senator Bourne; "Was there any held on the maiden voyage of the Titanic"?

Mr Andrews; "No, sir".

Senator Bourne; "Was there any notice of any drill"?

Mr Andrews; "That I do not know, sir".

Senator Bourne; "You saw none"?

Mr Andrews; "No, sir".

Senator Bourne; "You know that no drills were held"?

Mr Andrews; "Yes, sir".

Senator Bourne; "If there had been, you would have had to participate"?

Mr Andrews; "Yes, sir".

Senator Bourne; "And you would have been censured for not being at the drill if one was held"?

Mr Andrews; "Yes, Sir".

Senator Bourne; "Will you explain for the information of the committee what knowledge you have of what occurred immediately prior to and following the catastrophe of the Titanic"?

Mr Andrews; "Yes sir. I came off watch about a quarter to 11 and went down and turned in. About 20 minutes after that I was awakened up by a movement of the ship. Several of the boys woke up with the shock also. So with that I got out of my bunk and went into the working alleyway, seeing lots of stewards out. I walked up and down the alleyway several times with another steward. After that I went back to the quarters. I went back and laid down for a few minutes and then got up again. I had no sooner gotten there than somebody came and said", "All hands on deck".

Senator Bourne; "How severe was the shock? Did it awaken you? Were you asleep at the time"?

Mr Andrews; "I was just dozing off sir".

Senator Bourne; "Did it throw you out of your bunk"?

Mr Andrews; "No, sir".

Senator Bourne; "Did you think that the ship was in a serious condition at all"?

Mr Andrews; "No, sir; I thought something might have gone wrong with the engines".

Senator Bourne; "When you went out on deck, you assumed there was no danger, and went back to bed again, did you"?

Mr Andrews; "Yes, sir".

Senator Bourne; "Until the call came for "All hands on deck"?

Mr Andrews; "I got out of my bunk just before that, because I heard the rush of water, and I thought to myself, I guess I had better dress and go out; so I had just got to the door when somebody said", "All hands on deck".

Senator Bourne; "Now, will you go on"?

Mr Andrews; "With that I walked up on deck and stood by my boat. There were lots of people around, and I saw stores brought to the boat, and bread. I did not see the stores put in the boat. I assisted in helping the ladies and children into the boat. After the boat was full the officer called out for able seamen, or any individuals then, to man the boat. After several had got into the boat –

Senator Bourne; "How many"?

Mr Andrews; "6, sir. 5, sir, had got into the boat, and I was the sixth".

Senator Bourne; "5 besides yourself"?

Mr Andrews; "5 besides myself. The master-at–arms – there was two master-at-arms, and one was in charge of our boat".

Senator Bourne; "What was the name of the one in charge of your boat"?

Mr Andrews; "I do not know his name, sir; he was a master-at-arms".

Senator Bourne; "How many were passengers in the boat besides the six men manning the boat"?

Mr Andrews; "I should think about 50, sir".

Senator Bourne; "Was it one of the lifeboats or one of the collapsible boats"?

Mr Andrews; "A lifeboat".

Senator Bourne; "Now, will you go on"?

Mr Andrews; "After they were all in the boat the officer looked around at me and asked me if I could take an oar, and I said I could, sir. At that he told me to get into the boat. After I got in the boat I assisted by putting the rowlocks in. We lowered the boat to the water and rowed away from the ship. On our way out we came in contact with another boat, and stood by".

Senator Bourne; "That is, rested on your oars"?

Mr Andrews; "Yes, sir; we had to rest as we came across another boat, sir, filled up with ladies. The remark was passed by someone in the boat to go back, but as the two boats were full we stood at a distance away".

Senator Bourne; "Who passed the remark to go back"?

Mr Andrews; "One of the passengers, sir. The boats were full, sir".

Senator Bourne; "It was in the boat you were in, No 16 that one of the passengers passed this remark to go back"?

Mr Andrews; "Yes, sir".

Senator Bourne; "What attention did the officer in charge of the boat pay to the remark, if any"?

Mr Andrews; "I never heard nothing else, sir".

Senator Bourne; "Did the passenger that made the remark express any reason"?

Mr Andrews; "No, sir".

Senator Bourne; "He did not say why he wanted to go back"?

Mr Andrews; No, sir. "When daylight came we saw a light, which was on the Carpathia, and we proceeded to her".

Senator Bourne; "Did you see any light at the time of the accident, immediately, proceeding, from any ship, or any light of any kind or description other than what was on the Titanic itself"?

Mr Andrews; "Well, sir, we saw a light that seemed over the Titanic, back of the titanic".

Senator Bourne; "Did you think it was on the Titanic or beyond the Titanic"?

Mr Andrews; "No, sir. The Coxswain of the boat, the master-at-arms, thought it was another ship coming up to give assistance; but after a while the light disappeared".

Senator Bourne; "How long was that after you left the Titanic"?

Mr Andrews; "About an hour".

Senator Bourne; "That you saw this light over and beyond the Titanic"?

Mr Andrews; "Yes, sir".

Senator Bourne; "Believing it to be a rescue ship"?

Mr Andrews; "Yes, sir".

Senator Bourne; "You left the Titanic at what time – about what time – according to your recollection"?

Mr Andrews; "I should think it was about half past 12, sir".

Senator Bourne; "What time did the accident take place"?

Mr Andrews; "Well, sir, to my recollection, about 20 minutes past 11, sir".

Senator Bourne; "You were in your bunk at the time"?

Mr Andrews; "I was, sir".

Senator Bourne; "Are you absolutely sure as to the time of the accident or is that an impression"?

Mr Andrews; "Well, that is, so far as I know, sir, because I was in my bunk. There was no clock about. I think I was lying down about 20 minutes".

Senator Bourne; "You were dozing at the time of the accident, and so your idea of the exact time of the accident would be rather hazy, a mere guess. More of a guess than anything specific

Mr Andrews; "Yes".

Senator Bourne; "Will you kindly go on"?

Mr Andrews; "We transferred one of our men to the other boat".

Senator Bourne; "Why"?

Mr Andrews; "To assist to row. They had not very many in the other boat to row, sir".

Senator Bourne; "Did you transfer any of your passengers?

Mr Andrews; "No, sir; one of our crew, sir".

Senator Bourne; "Your boat was lowered past the steerage quarters, on a lower deck, was it not"?

Mr Andrews; "Well, it was the after boat on that side, so far as I know, sir, on the boat deck".

Senator Bourne; "In lowering it, it went by the steerage quarters, on the lower deck, did it not"?

Mr Andrews; "Yes, sir".

Senator Bourne; "Was there any effort on the part of the steerage men to get into your boat"?

Mr Andrews; "No, sir; I was told by the officer to allow nobody in the boat after the last one in it".

Senator Bourne; "Was there any effort of the part of anyone to get into it"?

Mr Andrews; "No, sir; everything was quiet, sir".

Senator Bourne; "When the officer started to fill the boat with the passengers, and the men to man the boat, were there any individuals who tried to get into the boat that he would not permit to get in"?

Mr Andrews; "No, sir".

Senator Bourne; "Was there any confusion or panic in loading the boat"?

Mr Andrews; "No, sir; none whatsoever".

Senator Bourne; "Kindly proceed".

Mr Andrews; "On the way to the Carpathia we saw some of our boats also proceeding. When we arrived there, there were one or two boats set adrift".

Senator Bourne; "Who set them adrift, and why"?

Mr Andrews; "That I do not know sir. I think they were damaged boats, sir".

50

Senator Bourne; "Well, of your knowledge, after they were filled and loaded, had any of their occupants been drowned or injured"?
Mr Andrews; "Not that I know of, sir".
Senator Bourne; "Your boat was as full as it would hold with safety, was it"?
Mr Andrews; "Yes, sir".
Senator Bourne; "You were up to the limit of your capacity"?
Mr Andrews; "I should think so, sir"
Senator Bourne; "Did you hear any cries"?
Mr Andrews; "Yes, sir".
Senator Bourne; "At the time that the ship sank"?
Mr Andrews; "Yes, sir".
Senator Bourne; "Immediately, proceeding or just following?
Mr Andrews; Well, sir, we had just stood by the other boat when we heard the cries".
Senator Bourne; "How far were you from the Titanic at the time"?
Mr Andrews; "I should say about half a mile, sir".
Senator Bourne; "Did you see the Titanic sink"?
Mr Andrews; "Well, sir, she must have been halfway sinking when I saw her".
Senator Bourne; "Did you hear any explosion or noise"?
Mr Andrews; "I heard just a small sound, sir; it was not very loud, but just a small sound".
Senator Bourne; "Did it create any discussion in the boat"?
Mr Andrews; "No, sir".
Senator Bourne; "What was the impression it made on your mind"?
Mr Andrews; "I thought perhaps it was one of the boilers that had

just gone, sir".

Senator Bourne; "Did you think that the ship broke in two"?

Mr Andrews; "That I do not know, sir. When we got away in the boat at the last everything seemed to go to a black mist. All the lights seemed to go out and everything went black".

Senator Bourne; "Did the lights go out altogether on the whole ship, or go out in part, and then the remainder go out"?

Mr Andrews; "They seemed to go out altogether, sir".

Senator Bourne; "You are familiar with the different decks of the ship? You know the E deck"?

Mr Andrews; "No, sir; I do not know them. I do not know anything about the decks, sir".

Senator Bourne; "E deck being the deck on which those quarters were located, was there any water on that deck, do you know"?

Mr Andrews; "Not as I know of, sir".

Senator Bourne; "That is all. We are very much obliged to you".

Witness excused.

Survivors

From an original photograph of Titanic survivor Charles Edward Andrews with his crewmates just after the Carpathia arrived in New York.

(British Pathe, Titanic disaster, still, 3:30)

Charlie's Promise

Following the Titanic Inquest, Charlie found it incredibly difficult to talk about the disaster. If the word ever arose he would quickly change the subject, for the deep scars in his mind and the delicate wounds of his emotions were far too painful.

After arriving back home in England, Charlie spent some much needed time at home with his family. Those following weeks after the Titanic's sinking, played terrific havoc on Charlie's mind, haunting him with horrendous nightmares. Still reeling in complete shock from the event, Charlie had also suffered discomfort from burning pains in his throat and chest caused by the freezing conditions. Over time Charlie's voice would change, as his larynx had sustained some degree of damage, contributed by the prolonged time out on the lifeboat, inhaling the dry icy sea air.

Nearing the end of his short recovery period, Charlie tried so hard to enjoy what time he had left with his family before returning to sea.

Over recent times, when Charlie happened to be home on leave, he had come to know a pretty young girl named Ivy. Ivy was about nine years old at the time, she often enjoyed playing outside on sunny days pushing her dolls pram in the front garden. When Charlie was out and about, he would occasionally walk by Ivy's garden gate, always baring his charming grin. Most of the time he would pleasantly assert a little fun with his light hearted manner. And other times would purposely pass a teasing remark at little sweet Ivy to provoke her always shy, but delightful smile.

But, as time passed, Charlie and Ivy subconsciously became harmoniously attuned with each other, regardless of the ten year age gap between them. As their unique friendship formed, Charlie felt confident, seeing something good and potentially special in Ivy, which he kept very secretly to himself.

Charlie's special secret in consequence, shaped his distant insights, and shortly before returning to sea, Charlie decided to take the challenge and make Ivy a beautiful promise. Charlie promised Ivy that he would wait however long it took for her to grow up. Then, when the time came and if she was ready, he would marry her! Charlie was fully aware of the fact that he was taking a huge chance. But whatever the outcome, it would be some years ahead in the future, before Charlie would know the outcome of his promise.

Before setting himself off for Southampton docks to return to sea, Charlie made a point of visiting the Solent shoreline in Southampton with his painful thoughts to pay his private respects to his cousin George, who drowned during the disaster and was later buried at sea.

George Edward Thomas Roberton

Written by Erik Roberton

This poem was dedicated to Erik's uncle: George Edward Thomas after he was tragically lost during the Titanic disaster.

George Edward Thomas Roberton
One of few to get a berth
His mother's breast had caused to
Swell with pride
Then this, the great unsinkable
Flags flying, ribbons barking
In 1912

George Edward Thomas Roberton
Was 18
In 2006
Still is
Still anchored silently alone
Fathoms deep, even deeper,
How long before his signet
Slipped from fleshless bone

George Edward Thomas Roberton
Sailed on the ebbing tide
Into the silt of screaming souls
Which now the reaper owns
Watertight doors closed in
Stern came up

George Edward Thomas Roberton
Went down
In town
The curtains were drawn
From chapel to Millbrook
D …parents lived on and lived on
In their other sons….and died
With their pride.
Yet he is as he was
Immortal this one,

George Edward Thomas Roberton
Her son.

Back To Sea

Three months after the sinking of Titanic, Charlie was back on the high seas working on the RMS Oceanic as a steward. Although the shock of the disaster was deep, Charlie's courage prevailed, leading him to reign on. The Steamship Oceanic was a regular voyage for Charlie until he signed on to the Royal Mail Steamship Edinburgh Castle on the 9th October 1912, sailing from Southampton to Cape Town in Africa. On the 26th December 1912, he was back serving again on the Oceanic as a steward until the 16th June 1913 when he then signed onto the Steamship Majestic for three trips. Charlie continued serving on various ships as steward or waiter until the First World War in 1914 when his position changed from serving passengers to serving allied troops.

In August, 1926 Charlie's closest brother Harry, married Iris Hughes, and like Charlie, Harry also found his dream following the sea as an able seaman. Harry served on fine ships such as the Berengaria during 1924; he also served on the Bat Castello, the Olympic, The Mauritania and in 1930 Harry served as personal steward to Prince George, Duke of Kent for the one voyage from Southampton to New York. As a token of appreciation, the stewards including Harry, each received a beautiful pocket watch with the royal crown engraved on the reverse.

After the war ended, Charlie was soon back serving as steward or first class waiter to passengers on his familiar ships and a few other similar liners up until the early 1930's.

By now Charlie's escalating popularity had spread throughout many ships, countless crew and returning passengers had become quite acquainted with him. Charlie found the tips were excellent, and most people tipped Charlie well, especially the regular passengers. However, Charlie soon discovered the crafty tricks that the rich would play to fool the stewards, especially the younger or inexperienced ones. Most parties would do almost anything to avoid paying a tip! One of the popular and most effective tricks often used was during the times they would send the serving steward back on board to fetch a forgotten item. After realising there was no forgotten item, the curious steward would have returned to the quayside to find his party had made a sharp exit and had quickly disappeared. Charlie had gotten used to the many scams he himself was a victim of, but over the years he had gotten used them, it never bothered him anymore, in fact some of his wages with tips combined, were more than Captain Edward Smith!

In 1932 when Charlie was thirty nine, something in the back of his mind kept on nagging him during his on-shore leave in Southampton.

He had always remembered a special promise he had made, way back in 1912, and had yet to fulfill.

The time had eventually come to see if his pretty childhood sweetheart, Ivy - now a young lady - had hopefully remembered his special promise he had made to her just two decades ago.

Back then, Charlie took a huge chance on his luck with a wonderful proposal, promising Ivy that when she had grown into a young woman, and if she was ready at the time - Charlie would marry her. But by now, many years later, however slim the chances were, Charlie still remained confident. If there was a special time in Charlie's life that he was more than ready to proceed with, it would be right now.

Charlie kept an impressive sparkling engagement ring close at hand and as a man of his word, he soon found the perfect place to fulfill his hopeful promise to Ivy, then the delicate moment followed as Charlie finally proposed!

Charlie couldn't believe his luck to find that Ivy had actually waited all those years for her precious promise, from her amazing friend who she had always liked. Remembering clearly the times he befriended her with amusement, over the garden gate, and most of all she had never forgotten his charming smile.

Amazingly, on the 26th of November 1932, Charlie married Ivy Winifred Powell, born 1st January, 1903 after some twenty years of waiting. It was a wonderful and joyous day for Charlie as his incredibly long awaited sweetheart finally became his wife. Charlie was so ecstatically happy, he was now sailing on cloud nine!

Charlie and Ivy on their wedding day in 1932

In August 1934 Charlie and Ivy had their first child, a daughter, Ann Marina. Charlie's wife Ivy was one of eight children born to parents Ann Nicklen born 1868, in Fordingbridge, Hampshire, and Albert William Powell born 1864 in Shirley, Southampton, he was a baker, the couple married in 1885.

Before Charlie joined the Queen Mary, he particularly enjoyed working aboard The Queen Elizabeth for a while as a Swimming Instructor. Charlie thought it was great; the man was living his dream, having fun times in the pool, working on fantastic ships, sailing across beautiful vast blue oceans, and most important a sense of belonging to a lovely family he could always look forward to coming back home to.

Sometimes when things didn't go too well back at home in England, they would usually turn out to be a good thing when Charlie was around. He would always hope that he could take good memories like those, back to sea with him to help keep him going.

On one such memorable occasion whilst on a short leave spell in Southampton, a day wasn't going particularly well for the family, when Charlie's mother-in-law, had an unfortunate accident; she had suffered quite a heavy tumble down the hard staircase, which left her shaken, but the fall had also caused some ugly bruising.

As chance would have it, Charlie happened to be visiting. And as usual, taking control, Charlie being Charlie took advantage of his handy massage techniques, humouring her at the same time with his tales of the sea. He began to massage the bruising, as he had done so many times before to many others on the ships; mind you it did hurt a lot, but eventually it was worth every moment, for afterwards the bruising had practically gone!

RMS Queen Mary

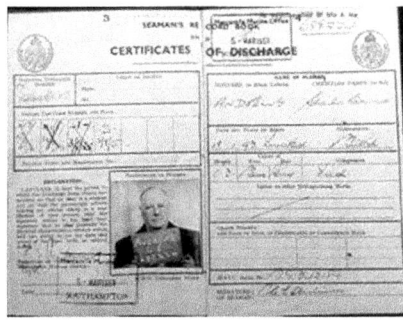

Charlie's Discharge Book For The RMS Queen Mary

In 1936, Charles Edward Andrews signed on to the RMS Queen Mary. The Cunard-White Star liner built in Clydebank, Scotland, was another fine ship that would bring Charlie to New York from Southampton with regularity. Docking at the Chelsea Piers, Charlie would enjoy his temporary onshore leave. During his time ashore Charlie liked to socialise and enjoyed spending time in New York. For most of his seafaring years out on the Queen Mary, Charlie mainly served as a waiter, masseur and Turkish bath attendant. Over passing years Charlie met many well-known people aboard the Queen Mary ship. Some of his most memorable moments shared with them included the times he swam with Gracie Fields in the ships pool, and as a masseur, massaged Tony Curtis along with many other well-known personalities. Charlie also enjoyed and valued the most amusing times in the saloon chatting to Tony Curtis and also Victor Mature. Charlie would watch the humorous stars merrily line up the tots of whiskies along the bar, and hearing them say "down the hatch" before knocking each one back!

In particular, Charlie's most valued memorable moments,
were during the many swimming sessions
shared with legendary swimmer, Johnny Weissmuller – of Tarzan fame -
aboard the Aquitania.

In 1937 back at home in England celebrations were in order again as Ivy gave birth to their second child, a son, John Edward. Balancing a family with a career at sea wasn't easy, but Charlie managed to do both, even though it had its disadvantages. He missed his family terribly, but he would always keep in touch, making sure they were well supported.

World War Two broke out in 1939; the Queen Mary served as a troop transporter for the military. The ship was heavily altered to accommodate thousands of allied troops, transporting them to Europe from the United States. The Queen Mary ship was given a camouflaged coating of grey paint to help blend against the grey seas. As Charlie continued to serve as steward - just as he did through the First World War - he would enjoy serving the troops as opposed to civilian passengers.

The Queen Mary Steamship had it tough out on the sea during the war, not only was she a high risk target stalked by u-boats but she sustained some damage when in October 1942 she was cut up in her own path by the British cruiser, the Curacao. This in turn caused the Queen Mary to slice the cruiser in two. The cruisers grave mistake caused a loss of more than three hundred lives. However, although the Queen Mary sustained some damage to her bow, she could not stop to help, for it was far too risky and dangerous. That same year, in December when the Queen Mary was South of Greenland transporting thousands of troops, she hit a nasty storm. The Queen Mary took a mighty rough ride through the North Atlantic Ocean that day. She creaked loud and groaned with the movement, as she was shaken and tossed around from all sides. Then from nowhere, a rogue wave of almost thirty metres high rolled towards her and slammed into her side causing her to tilt a staggering fifty two degrees. The crew and troops were thrown around, amid everything else. Water was everywhere, in the cabins, pouring through broken ports. But had she gone another three degrees, the Queen Mary would have capsized altogether and all on board would most probably have perished, including Charlie. However, the ship managed to settle slowly, righting herself, and with effort managed to steam back to port. A few casualties escaped with minor injuries. Charlie was always aware of the dangers at sea, especially during the war. Ships were sitting targets and many were lost at sea. The Queen Mary was a high risk ship, and Hitler wanted her destroyed. He had wanted her destroyed so badly, that he offered a reward of £250.000 to any of his men that would successfully sink her. At times, torpedoes were fired at the Queen Mary out at sea during the war, but luckily she was never hit. Her impressive speed certainly contributed a great deal to her protection. Could the Queen Mary have been protected by some kind of magical force? You could quite easily have imagined she was, for she seemed so invincible. During the war, The Queen Mary Trooper did look the part with her haunting grey "ghost" appearance, while docked between naval ships at the New York piers. On either side, allied warships would constantly protect her from possible air attacks.

Between the late forties and fifties during the McCarthy Era, at the time when America took a tough stand on the threat of communism, entering the Country proved more difficult, for everyone had to be thoroughly checked before they were allowed in. Charlie's brother Harry's son, Raymond Andrews - another fine seaman of the Andrews family, serving for the Royal Navy - had just stepped from his ship, HMS Sheffield at the New York Piers. He noticed the Queen Mary was in port, docked on the other side of the pier and so walked over to see if Charlie was about. As Ray walked up the gangplank to enter the fine Queen Mary steamship, he wondered if anyone would know of Charlie's whereabouts. And with that question in mind, Ray walked on board further and approached a seaman on watch, to ask him if he would know anything of Charlie. By the huge grin on the seaman's face, without a doubt, he definitely knew Charlie. The seaman then kindly arranged for someone to take Ray further aboard the luxurious Queen Mary liner to find him.

Charlie's Nephew; Raymond Andrews

It was the first time the relatives had met up together at the New York piers, so they took advantage of the chance to catch up on some gossip over a pint.

On approaching the crowds at the exit gates, seamen and military personnel began queuing, ready with their papers and documents at hand for checking. But when Charlie's turn came, the familiar faced security men just gave a warm smile asking Charlie how his trip was, and then let him pass straight through, unchecked! Astonished, Ray turned to Charlie and asked" How is it that you managed to get through so easily"? Charlie beamed with his confident charming smile, and replied, "I've been coming through here since 1908 and everyone local here, knows me very well"!

He was right; New York played a big part in Charlie's life. And as the two relatives walked together further, Ray could see how familiar Charlie's face had become to the local people of New York City. Just like in the days when he was a familiar young lad waiting at the Liverpool piers for his father Henry to return from sea. It was in a way quite touching to be happening again, and this time it was happening practically on the other side of the world! Ray was just amazed, as almost everyone in the vicinity would acknowledge Charlie as he passed by. The complete area seemed to be bustling with activity as men passed back and forth through the security gates of the piers. Several local policemen out on the beat would always ask after Charlie. The familiar drivers sat in their handy cabs waiting for fares, would peer up over their newspapers and respond to Charlie with a cheerful nod!

Charlie liked to go to, "the meeting place of the world", Jack Dempsey's bar in New York City. It was typical of Charlie to visit Jack's bar as, being an Irish pub they sold his favourite tipple; Guinness. I can understand why Charlie loved it there so much. It was a very popular hang out with tired seamen and military personnel, the perfect place to relax, conversing over a pint.

Throughout the forties and fifties, Charlie had got used to venturing around New York City, a place sometimes menaced with crime and wrongdoing. During those hazardous times cultural pressures began brewing throughout the neighbourhoods of New York City between rival gangs. Violent crimes and conflicts proved a hellish nightmare for the innocent people of New York, making it sometimes unsafe to wander out onto the streets

A frightening event occurred on one of those particular days when the strains of criminal minds had taken their toll. Charlie was out for his usual leisurely walk stretching his sea legs, minding his own business. He had then stepped into a public phone booth to make a regular call, but on doing so he felt uneasy and sensed trouble. Whilst glancing out onto the street, Charlie recognised a distinct car cruising by very slow. As it drew closer, Charlie had had to take a second look to confirm for real, what he had seen! The occupants were fierce looking gangsters, whom happened to be gazing in his direction, armed with what looked like machine guns!

With instinct panic and fear setting in, Charlie automatically found himself caught up in the line of fire between two rival gangs. As he swiftly shielded himself deep inside the phone booth as far as he could from the gunfire, his mind instantly recalled the dreadful thoughts and feelings of his horrifying Titanic ordeal. Those abrupt moments seemed like forever as Charlie closed his eyes until it was quiet again.

Feeling greatly relieved, Charlie cautiously checked the street to see if the car had gone. The street was remarkably quiet, but although Charlie felt quite shaken, he knew he was alright.

And as luck would have it for yet another time, again Charlie's life was miraculously saved, evidently shielded by the hardwood frame of the phone booth! After the shock of it all, he no doubt returned straight back to the safety of Jack's bar for another pint! I would guess by now Charlie was probably wondering if he was actually born with nine Lives!

Sometimes there were many occasions when Charlie felt much safer being back at his home in southern England, where he would spend precious times with his wife Ivy. But even those innocent times out together didn't always go to plan, such as a time on one gloomy evening when the film "A Night to Remember" premiered in Southampton, in 1958.

Charlie decided to brave the chance and take his wife Ivy out to watch the movie. Although he was looking forward to the evening out with his wife, he was also secretly dreading the film.

A little later during the disaster part of the movie, Charlie felt rather uncomfortable with some of the scenes. He had no idea the film would start to have such an effect on him. Feeling alarmed by the terrible emotions beginning to surface from within, Charlie tried hard to ignore them. But it was useless; the final stages of panic took control as his heart started to race rapidly. Charlie's powerful anxiety attack increased into an uncomfortable sweat of fear. The feelings were so overwhelming Charlie had to get up and leave the theatre. He never watched the film again.

There never seemed to be enough time to share together, as the time would come around yet again for Charlie to return to his ship. However, by now Charlie was really looking forward to a long retirement.

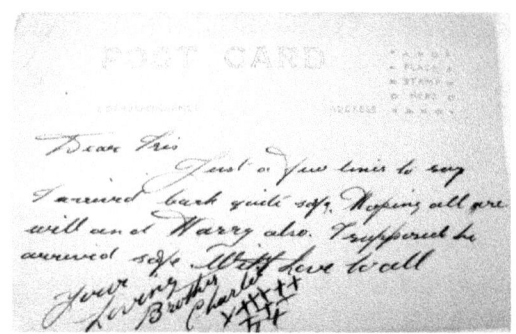

Charlie's beautiful handwriting
as show on one of his many postcards, received back home.

Retirement

Celebrations were in order again when; Charlie and Ivy's daughter Ann Marina married Ivan Garbett, in 1957. They went on to have one daughter, Debra born in 1959. In the same year, Charlie finally retired from his long exhausting maritime career and now looked forward to spending a well deserved retirement with his wife Ivy. There was indeed plenty of living to catch up on, making up time for the many years they had missed together during the times Charlie was away at sea.

Whenever the chance arose, my grandparents' would always pop out to their favourite local pub; The Salisbury Arm's just situated on the corner of their street - in Shirley - probably not even a hundred yards from their garden gate. Just like a new couple, Charlie and Ivy would sit for an evening, over a few pints of Guinness, taking an interest in listening to each other's stories from the times they were apart. However, over the years Ivy had noticed the distinct changes in Charlie's voice. By now, his voice had weakened to almost a whisper, damaged from a combination of inhaling the icy sea air, and shock from the Titanic disaster. Luckily it wasn't serious, but it still constantly reminded Charlie and his family of that terrible day.

Finally being together, made such a difference in Charlie and Ivy's lives. They would devote time to share the simplest things in life, such as watching a good movie at the cinema, eating out at their favourite places, walking their cute scruffy little dog Rex around town, and browsing through the shops.

Whenever they both socialised out somewhere, Ivy would always dress smart, taking pride in her appearance, she always looked her best. Ivy and Charlie shared a good deal in common; above all, they both shared a passion for a regular bet on the horses.

My grandparents would plan special days out together, in particular travelling by coach to their favourite places - normally racecourses - to enjoy a flutter on the favourites. Times were good and my grandparents were just starting to have fun, valuing every moment shared. The little things in life seemed all that were needed to keep them happy. Although life appeared to be going well for Charlie and his wife, little did they realise that their blissful times together would be taken away so soon. Just as Charlie had endured forty five years of hard work at sea, he was one of those who would unfortunately go on to have only a few years of retirement to enjoy.

Death

One wet wintery afternoon in December, Charlie and Ivy decided to have some fun out, daring the miserable weather as they had done so, on many occasions. Getting away from the humdrum of home for a bit, regardless of the wind and pouring rain, the couple eagerly left their home in Romsey Road to take their regular walk through their home town of Shirley. They both had fun popping into the bookmakers for a quick bet, and then afterwards spent some time visiting the shops for a browse, for some last bits of Christmas shopping! Full of high spirits, they then both made a dash for a refreshment, risking the venture furthermore against the gloomy elements!

The rain persisted, pelting down hard on the huge glass windows of the local cafe, as Charlie and Ivy sat together chatting to some of the regulars and familiar faces over a most welcome steaming hot cup of tea.

The time had seemingly passed by rather quickly after my grandparents had enjoyed conversing about the dismal weather and other trivial matters, but by the time they both finished the final dregs at the bottom of their teacups, they were almost ready to face the soggy walk home. The weather remained pitiful and began to worsen still as the afternoon gradually darkened into a depressing early evening. On the way back towards home, battling on through the strong gusts of wind and torrential rain, Ivy looked at Charlie's sopping wet face, and developed another idea. Just before, they would finally reach home, Charlie and Ivy both happily agreed to nip into the Salisbury Arms, for a quick Christmas tipple, and as usual both ordered a favourite pint of Guinness.

Time would never seem to give them enough hours in the day for it always flashed by far too quickly, although by now it really was time for the couple to return home for dinner. The last few moments challenging the poor weather conditions had finally come, but by the time they had hurried the hundred yards or so home from the pub, they were both feeling pretty drenched and quite cold, not that it bothered Charlie that much, he was used to the elements.

The thoughts of a hot home cooked dinner always made it feel great to get back home, but best of all were the thoughts of getting warm again as they snuggled up cosy in front of the open log fireside, full from a hearty meal!

Although the pair had only gone to their regular café after a browse around the town and returned home soaking wet, they had actually enjoyed the thrill of an afternoon in the rain. Come, snow, rain or shine, Charlie and Ivy knew how to make the best of passing their time, however close is was to home!

Gradually, though over the following few days, Charlie began to feel a bit stuffy and thought nothing of it, believing it was probably just a casual cold coming on. He also began to appear very tired combined too with profound feelings of fatigue. Although his symptoms lingered on, Charlie seemed unconcerned, but Ivy started to worry and so kept a close eye on him. Another few days had passed, and by now Charlie had felt so bad he decided to stay in bed. Although he was still feeling pretty rough, Charlie did enjoy the attentive care from his wife over the next few days or so as he continued to rest in bed. It wasn't long though, before a noticeably high fever began to take hold of Charlie, as something else more sinister was starting to develop. Ivy did her best to care for her poor Charlie while he lay in bed suffering. The situation had just turned for the worst, and by now Charlie could feel pains in his chest, especially when he coughed, a cough that Ivy suspected was a bit too severe to be normal, so with increased worry and as a precaution, she decided to call the doctor. Charlie was instantly admitted to hospital that day, where he was diagnosed with pneumonia, Charlie's outcome looked most unpromising as the predominant ailment prevailed. Soulful Ivy sat by Charlie's bedside on that New Year's afternoon of her birthday and held his hand. As she watched him sleeping, she began to reflect back in time, remembering all the special times they had shared together, times that Charlie had made particularly memorable for them both before his return to the sea. But most of all her mind would recall the amusement they shared over the garden gate when she was nine years old, but above all the special promise her brave seaman had made to her all those years ago. Gripped by her raw emotions, tears began to fill her big brown eyes as she gently kissed her husband Charlie goodnight. As tears began to roll down her cheeks - gently staining her perfect powdered face - Ivy began to pray desperately in her mind. Praying for him to recover, giving her another chance of many more years with her one and only – Charlie. Feeling reluctant to leave her Charlie's side, Ivy so wanted to stay, but time was passing and the day was becoming awfully late as the noticeably evening skies darkened outside the hospital windows. But, along with her discontent, Ivy managed to leave the hospital and made her way home.

As the following day emerged, the devastating news had come, Ivy then realised her prayers of faith had been far too late. Ivy was informed that her precious Charlie had sadly gone!

On the 2nd day of January in 1961, the day after Ivy's 58th birthday, Charlie took his last breath, passing peacefully away. It was all such a big shock; one minute he was fit as a fiddle out having fun and the next, he was gone! The family wondered if Charlie would have lived longer if he hadn't gone out in the rain that day. But who knows? Ironically, only one fact stood out. During most of Charlie's life he had been surrounded by water in one form or another. But who would have believed that the element of water, which played such a huge part in Charlie's dreams and ambitions, may have eventually contributed into taking his life. The regrettable day came to scatter Charlie's ashes in Stoneham Cemetery, in Southampton. It was a very sad day for Ivy and her family. Charlie really didn't deserve to suffer and be taken so quickly, and so early during his retirement, which he was just beginning to enjoy. He should have had a long happy retirement, but missed out on so many joyful times with his wife, two children, three grandchildren and nine great-grandchildren, including the day his son John Edward married Mary Freeman in 1962 at St James Church in Shirley, Southampton. Whom then, went on the have (me) their first daughter born in 1963, then my sister Jacqueline, born in 1964.

By leaving the legend of the fateful Titanic disaster in our family history, Charles Edward Andrews will never be forgotten. This brave and highly admirable man well earned his right for recognition; Charlie touched so many lives during his career at sea and through this book will continue to touch the lives of his many future generations.

An Ode To A Seaman

Written By Aston Cerexhe

In those days times were tough
On people trying to get by
For Charlie growing up was rough
But he managed with strong family ties

Here is a lad with the sea in his blood
His father a seaman and brothers too
It would make his family very proud
A career at sea for Charlie to pursue

So up he grew with thoughts of the sea
And went on to follow the steps of his dad
With many a visit to quay after quay
Not knowing that one day it would all turn bad

In 1912 on that terrible day
A nightmare did ensue
The ship did sink and fall to lay
Shortly after two

The heavens looked after Charlie that night
And ordered him to row a boat
To reassure people from fear and fright
He did so proudly with lumps in his throat

Of strong character and sound mind
Charlie still pursued that career at sea
Many ties to the ocean he did bind
And hopes for his safety he had to plea

For many more good years
Charlie sailed the high seas
Making many friends over a chat and a beer
But then had a family to please

Charlie now has children and a wife
And looks to a happy retirement
To settle down away from sea life
For a few good years of merriment

And so Charlie's end is near
After life at sea made his horizons wide
He went on to cause many a tear
By contracting pneumonia – and died

Memorable Charlie

Charlie's Closest Brother; Harry Andrews

During 1993, Charlie's closest brother, Harry (pictured) fell ill; the illness had affected his mind, which by now had deteriorated to a certain degree. As a result, instead of realising he was in hospital, he believed he was in jail! And so with that belief he kept on asking the family to go and fetch Charlie to come and free him, saying that Charlie would know what to do! But of course Charlie had already gone years before and it was sad not being able to get Charlie for him. However, shortly afterwards Harry passed peacefully away.

81

May and Raymond Andrews

During some years later, Harry's son Raymond Andrews remembered a time when they were permanently returning home from Thailand, a country where he and his wife had been living for a while. On the ferry back home to England, a steward had got chatting to Ray whilst he was serving their meals and at some point during their conversation the steward mentioned he himself had worked aboard the RMS Queen Mary. With a spontaneous curiosity, Ray instantly asked the steward if he knew of his uncle Charlie. Surprised by the steward's reply Ray sat stunned as the steward suddenly started to react in amazement. It was as if the steward couldn't get his words out quick enough. Apparently, the steward quite definitely had known of Charlie and then he began to explain to Ray what a great character he thought he was and how other people highly regarded the man with the utmost of respect. He had also told Ray that Charlie was one of the longest serving men to have worked aboard the Queen Mary. Charlie must have left quite an impression, as after the conversation Ray and his wife May were surprisingly both treated like royalty!

Acknowledgements & Credits

With special thanks to;

My Wonderful Mother - Mary Andrews
Superb Support - Raymond Andrews
My Appreciation - Brian Osborne
Cheers Dude - Richie Bentley
My Kind Mother-In-Law - Dorothy Holdford
Mel & Phil Walters - From The Woodburningcentre.Com In
Drimoleague
Matthew & Jamie - My wonderful helpful and supportive son's
Erik Roberton – For the kind use of his poem
Robert Andrews – For Extra Info/Photos
Aston – Thank you hubby for the fantastic poem you wrote
especially for Charlie, the endless supply of tea and the
encouragement that kept me going!

Credits
British Pathe, Titanic disaster (still 3:30)
Testimony of C E Andrews (Am.Inq, P622)

Extra
I wish to add an extra thank you
to my lovely mother Mary and second cousin Raymond Andrews
for their outstanding input, patience and time

Art, Illustrations & Design

Book Cover Design & Illustrations; Marina Andrews

All Internal Sketches; Marina Andrews

Titanic/Iceberg Collision Painting; Marina Andrews

SS Majestic Painting; Mary Andrews

About The Author

On a Good Friday, in the spring month of April in 1963, a first child was born to proud parents Mary and John Andrews. They named their bonny, blue eyed, daughter Marina.

Marina Andrews began her life with her parents at her Grandparent's house living in the southern Maritime city of Southampton. When Marina reached twenty months of age, her only sister Jacqueline was born. Beginning school at the tender age of five appeared daunting for Marina, but by the time she had reluctantly settled into school life the family moved home. Finding life at her new school much less stressful, Marina settled progressively well into a more modern school. During her junior school years, Marina discovered a passion for sketching; valuing her own time, she spent many hours improving her much loved talent. When Marina was sixteen, she left school, days later her grandmother (Charlie's wife, Ivy) passed away peacefully at their home. After several years in employment, Marina married in 1983 and became a mother to eight wonderful children; Matthew, Victoria, Rebecca, Jamie, Jessica,

Robert, Lewis, and Rachelle. During this time Marina expanded her artistic skills from sketching to painting and now sees herself as a budding artist. In 1999 her marriage dissolved, ending in divorce. In April 2004 Marina re-married also gaining three step-daughters; Alicia Danielle and Mercedes. Marina is also a grandmother to nine grandchildren; Kurt, Ella, Leah, Joshua, Oscar, Jake, Melody, Jack and Marley.

www.ingramcontent.com/pod-product-compliance
Ingram Content Group UK Ltd.
Pitfield, Milton Keynes, MK11 3LW, UK
UKHW021326290825
7642UKWH00022B/180